Noah built the first houseboat.

Cleopatra floated down the Nile
on a houseboat.

CAPRA PRESS TITLES
DEALING WITH WESTERN MAN IN WATER:

HOT TUBS, Leon Elder [*new Vintage edition*]
FREE BEACHES, Elder & Crawford
GREAT HOT SPRINGS OF THE WEST, Bill Kaysing
WATER SQUATTERS, Beverly Dubin

Water Squatters

The Houseboat Lifestyle

A DOCUMENTARY OF HANDMADE HOUSES AFLOAT, WITH PHOTOGRAPHS
MAINLY FROM SAUSALITO, SEATTLE, THE SACRAMENTO DELTA,
AND FOREIGN LANDS, WITH INFORMATION ON MARINAS,
GALLEY RECIPES FEATURING HOUSEBOAT SOUP, HOW
TO COPE WITH CHILDREN AND ANIMALS ABOARD,
REMEMBERING THAT IT ALL BEGAN WITH NOAH

by

Beverly Dubin

with drawings by

Bill Oetinger

CAPRA PRESS   1975   SANTA BARBARA

This book is dedicated to the memory of my mother Beatrice Winograd Dubin.

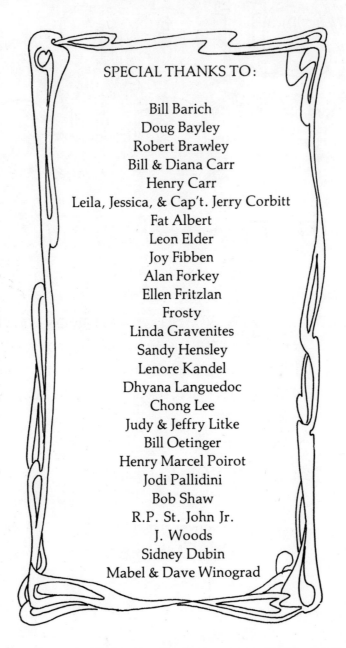

SPECIAL THANKS TO:

Bill Barich
Doug Bayley
Robert Brawley
Bill & Diana Carr
Henry Carr
Leila, Jessica, & Cap't. Jerry Corbitt
Fat Albert
Leon Elder
Joy Fibben
Alan Forkey
Ellen Fritzlan
Frosty
Linda Gravenites
Sandy Hensley
Lenore Kandel
Dhyana Languedoc
Chong Lee
Judy & Jeffry Litke
Bill Oetinger
Henry Marcel Poirot
Jodi Pallidini
Bob Shaw
R.P. St. John Jr.
J. Woods
Sidney Dubin
Mabel & Dave Winograd

LIBRARY OF CONGRESS CATALOGING IN PUBLICATION DATA

Dubin, Beverly.
  Water Squatters.

  Bibliography: p.
  1. House-boats.   I. Title.
GV836.D82   797.1'2   75-6693
ISBN 0-88496-020-X

Capra Press
631 State Street
Santa Barbara, California 93101

Each houseboat has a
story to tell . . . though the
people may not be there.

"Houseboating is a state of mind." —Henry

FOREWORD

Beverly Dubin has that gift of getting there, and surely could drive her van through the eye of a needle, twists through Sunday traffic like somebody's version of Neal Cassidy, behind giant dark glasses and blowing dark hair, her durable Nikon bouncing in the glove compartment and me clutching the dashboard handle. It was a clear October Sunday and she was taking me to see with my own eyes. Out over the Golden Gate, sails as frequent as whitecaps, to see the water squatters of Sausalito. I had already seen her first photographs and read an early draft of this book, but had no idea how big it all really was, how extensive. I thought she was dealing with a few hardy souls here and there on the edges of our land who had the dream and forebearance to live afloat, like early land squatters who had the ingenuity to make a life on water, to build private environments as they damned well pleased and with no idea of really going anywhere except to list a bit with tide and current and tie down crockery in a storm. Which is to say I wasn't prepared—for Beverly, her unholy driving, or what she had to show me.

We took the natives' old road into Sausalito, off the freeway at the north end on dirt and ruts, and slid down curves to the water. There she slowed down and began to show me all that was there.

I saw, not a few isolated craft, but a whole world in faint motion— hundreds of dwellings stretched-out as far as I could see—all of them listing in unison with something that goats, capricorns, and landlubbers don't usually think about—water. We parked, got out and began to walk. I slowly absorbed this marvelous madness, this floating city where the lids were off, where the conformity levied by building codes, taxes and developers, by planners, officialdom and cosigned rubber stamps; where all these things, including sidewalks, gutters, parks, playgrounds and streetlamps, had been totally disavowed. Floating people, living their own ways—in revolt, madness, triumph and freaky improvisation. It took an hour or more just to walk the perimeter and get the impact of what had happened behind our backs, what a special reality had been created.

For you who have lived like me, with boundaries and stakes, sod to dig in and trees to plant that might someday tower above our houses, this was something else. These were the water squatters who either despise, hate or can't afford pavement, and who seek a last freedom in being afloat, and use air [encapsulated in hulls and oil drums], instead of concrete, to give them a hold. Air and water. I was awed. I saw transplanted two-story frame houses gently rocking, waving towers, and an array of architectural spectacles, mutant structures, nightmares and glories, slipshod here, triumphant there, globular, boxy, wild, humble, absurd and shanty cozy. It was the most disparate cluster of dwellings that could ever be, and all of it, because it was a calm day, in the very scarcest motion. People are not that different. Stand back from a crowd and they all look pretty much the same. Differences in height, weight, age and complexion aren't really very dramatic. But behold what comes from their minds and hands! A houseboat bulging with plexiglass eyes stared at us with Martian inscrutability. Unnerving. "And this," said Beverly, "is only the beginning of it. Wait till you see the Delta, and Seattle and Miami and Maine."

I was startled. Not that some of the places didn't look like garbage dumps, but that directly alongside would be something majestic, proud, weird or poetic. Water is amorphous, so is the cosmos. Not easy for a goat to admit, or to feel at ease with.

"Hey!" said Beverly, pointing, "Look at that." We backtracked a quarter mile and hurried out on a dock past a grandiose houseboat with studio windows, quadrophonic chamber music and nodding houseplants. We reached a heavy old cargo ship with a pair of weather-beaten masts, knotted and checked like old telephone poles. The hull was white, the caulking and planking rough and calloused. The schooner Isabel. She sat heavy and strong in the water, not in the light, dainty way that yachts have. A pert little woman was sunning on the main hatch, knees drawn up under her chin, eyes closed. A girl and a sheep dog were romping alongside. They were obviously at home. If I had been alone, I probably would have passed by with a wave and smile, but as I said, Beverly gets there.

That your ship?" she called, and when the woman graciously nodded, more questions followed and gradually a conversation took shape. This turned out to be the home of Steve and Judy Siskind, their three children, a dog and cat. It was Danish built in 1913 and plied the North Sea with cargoes of salt, ore and grain. They hocked everything to buy it, and sailed it back to the West Coast five years ago and began outfitting the empty hull into comfortable rooms with a piano, couches, bookshelves, rugs and hanging ferns. Now they were free to be almost anywhere—a season in the Grenadines, a year in San Diego, a visit in Santa Barbara, a long lay-over in Sausalito. Steve appeared and invited us below. We listened to his ideologies. He is an architect and planner.

"In the first place," he said, "anyone who lives on water is a bit unusual. The ocean offers our last freedom. Land has been assaulted and insulted. Man has brought ruination upon it. Now we're beginning to exploit the sea and make the same mistakes we made on land. Territorial lines are being drawn further out at sea as though each country has the right to dredge it to death, or use it as a garbage dump. Along the shore, slums are being created

by haphazard marinas. Look up the road at Gate 5. There're 400 houseboats jammed together there without privacy, their sewage spilling onto the mudflats. You need a gas mask when the tide is low. Any marine life that survives around there is poisoned. Worse than any tract development I've ever seen, and they're bad enough. No one is taking responsibility for sanitation or space or the survival of the sea itself. What freedom is there when we are infecting the very element we live on? Yet with a little foresight, cooperation and simple technology, it could be a paradise."

Steve was obviously an intense and dedicated man, a "bit unusual", and with the courage to raise his family on this aged cargo ship. His neighbor, moored alongside, was a true houseboat aristocrat, his hold stoked with the best wines and brandies. When he came for dinner, he brought along a whole case of good vintage cabernet. In spite of the negative aspects of life afloat Steve described, he is busy doing something about it. He bought some marina land behind his dock and has the vision to design model facilities for people to live on water with space around them and compatible with the ecology of the sea. He founded the Environmental Planning Institute in Sausalito and is working with planners and city governments across the country.

"We ran into a big storm," Judy told Beverly. "The winds were hurricane force, 70 knots, and I was up on deck fighting it. We passed within fifty feet of a freighter that sank an hour later. I was terrified. At one point I went below to check on the kids. That was before we built the partitions and the hold was just one enormous room. And there I found them, during the height of the storm, singing, laughing and riding their bikes in circles. No one ever told them that people can die at sea, or that there are such things as seasickness and fear."

This is Beverly's book. It is entirely her vision of a way of life that may vanish in the next decade. She wanted to document it while it still flourished. But after meeting Steve Siskind, she sees that houseboat living may well proliferate, that more of mankind will settle on this watery frontier, as pioneers once filled the valleys of our land. She has an eye for the flamboyant, for the bizarre flowers from inventive minds. She saw too the patriarch in Steve, the stern wisdom. His cautions may contain the answer to the perpetuation of the very marvelous things that Beverly looks for.

If we think of the sea, and all that lives and grows in it, as an enormous mammal, we'll be considerate of its meanest mudflats and harbors, for these are the edges of its being. If it suffers our poisons, it would die under our hulls. It is entirely within our means to live well with her, and catch lively suppers off our decks.

—Leon Elder

"You have to work hard when you're anchored
out. You have to haul wood, water and
supplies to your boat."

CONTENTS

WATER SQUATTERS

This book is about houseboats and other small craft, that people live on. "Home on a houseboat or sailboat is a different, wonderful, unusually creative way to live. It is an alternative life-style to living in an apartment, flat, private home, truck or tipi. When the tide comes in, your home floats and moves about in the water. There is a gentle rocking if the water is calm, much more movement when it's rough and choppy. The tide goes out and your house settles into the sand and mud, maybe even slightly tilted to one side. Everything gets stowed carefully, and you put precious things in places where they can't fall. You adapt yourself and your things to living in a moving, floating place.

I hope this book comes in time to do some good for these people hanging onto the edge of America. Although my pictures are primarily West Coast, shot in Sausalito, Seattle and the Sacramento Delta, there are houseboat marinas all over the country, from Maine to Florida, and in the big rivers as well. Water being the common element, the problems and satisfactions of this lifestyle must be pretty much the same for all of them wherever they be.

"The Madonna," pictured on page 5 in its days of glory, burned to a skeleton a few days before Christmas, 1974, cause unknown. In January, 1975, after 20 years of struggle between the county of Marin and the houseboat dwellers of Richardson Bay, the Public Works Director ordered those occupying Kappas Marina to move to a new facility by mid-February. The county is prepared to tow away any floating home that does not comply. The $500,000 new facility is a tidy set of piers just a few hundred yards from the old marina, and is the first of five planned in the area. It offers connections for sewage, water, gas, telephone, television and electricity, along with paved parking lots, bicycle paths, paved streets and outdoor lighting. It's possibly the first planned floating home community in California.

But some of the houseboat people lament being pushed into a "well planned suburb." "They're killing a community," complained Jim Reardon, a veteran houseboater. He objects to the fact that the new harbor becomes a mudflat a few hours each day when the tide is out which would triple the deterioration of his hull, and the cost of a sewage pump (about $1000) that is required, while he figures an adequate pump should be no more than $250. Beyond that, the berth fees nearly double, from $80 to $150, and many of the houseboats are in no condition to be moved or brought "up to code."

It looks like the grand funk architecture, lifestyle afloat as we knew it, is coming to an end. I'm glad I photographed the pioneer architecture while it existed, before it turns into something else.

FINDING A HOUSEBOAT

Go out to the harbour and look around. There are many different kinds of boats and houseboats that people live on. Some houseboats are simple A-frames on a barge; others are elaborate handbuilt artistic architectural statements that float, and still others are funky little cabins built on abandoned hulls and barges, or out of old fishing boats. A lot of boats were used by Marines during the war as landing craft, and then abandoned. I know of some people who built a really nice houseboat inside an old submarine chaser, and another person who moved a freight-train caboose onto a barge and has made it his floating home. Use your imagination, there are endless possibilities for building your own houseboat, and numerous unique and exciting choices for renting or buying an already existing houseboat.

Check the various harbours for bulletin boards. Many people put up ads listing houseboats for rent or for sale. Ask the Harbour Master about any houseboats that may be available. If you want to move your own houseboat to the dock, this is also the person to ask about berth space, fees, and utilities that are available. Ideally the dock you tie up to should offer showers, toilet facilities, electricity, and a pay telephone. Look in the local newspapers for any current listings of houseboats being sold or leased, and ask the people that live on houseboats near-by for information about any houseboats they may know of that might be available.

". . . well, you wouldn't catch me living anywhere else, like in an apartment or anything. There's an incredible amount of stuff lying around to use, old boats . . . and anyway, it's hard to have houseboats in the desert." —Bill

"I live on the water because I don't like being near other people. I moved onto the boat to get away."

"It floats, so it's a boat . . . and it's a houseboat." —Jay

KEEPING AFLOAT

There are many things to consider when shopping for a houseboat; especially important is the condition of the bottom of the boat. After all, the most important thing is that it floats. There is a possibility of travel in some houseboats, but most are not sea-worthy—it is expensive to put an engine into an abandoned hull. Make sure the bottom of the boat is in good or repairable condition. Metal exposed to water will rust and most boats must be pulled out of the water every year or so to have the bottom scraped of barnacles and rust, and have the holes patched and painted with special marine latex paint. The paint costs about $80 per gallon. Marine latex paint will stop leakage and rust. It costs anywhere from $100 - $500 to haul a houseboat out of the water, depending on its size, the drydock you go to, and how long you keep the boat out of the water. There is also a fee for the space you park the boat on while you work on it.

Some houseboats are floated on big styrofoam blocks. These have to be replaced every few years because the styrofoam gets eaten away by algae. Styrofoam blocks can be purchased in 1' X 20' rectangles. You cut the styrofoam into blocks, swim underneath your boat and shove them into the spaces that have been eaten away by the algae. Houseboats can be floated on barges and pontoons, on big metal airtight containers, like oil drums, cement blocks, platforms built on styrofoam, and some are just built on old boats.

GENERAL MAINTENANCE

Check the bottom every year or two.

Check the bilge pump and make sure the bilge is pumped every month. All switches located in the bilges should be designed for submerged use. A manual bilge should be carried irrespective of any other pumping devices.

Check hull fittings and shut off valves. These should be easily accessible.

TOOLS AND SPARE PARTS

Spare batteries and spare bulbs for battery operated lights (remember you won't have electricity if you are anchored offshore)
First Aid Kit
Fire Extinguisher
Adjustable Wrenches (Crescent)
Pliers, Hammer, Various Screwdrivers, Phillips Screwdriver
Small Saw, Nails, Bolts, Screws
Miscellaneous lengths of Rope, nylon is best. Sea water will eventually eat away hemp rope.

The City Council of the City of Sausalito does ordain as follows:

Section 1: Definitions. For the purpose of this ordinance, the words and phrases herein defined shall be construed in accordance with the definitions set forth unless it is apparent from the context that a different meaning is intended:

(a) *Houseboat.* Any watercraft or industrial or commercial structure on or in the waters of the State, floating or nonfloating, which is designed or fitted out as a place of habitation and is not principally used for transportation. "Houseboat" includes platforms, and waterborne hotels and restaurants. "City or county" means any city, county, city and county, or port authority.

(b) *Houseboat Marina.* Any area within the City covered by the waters of San Francisco and Richardson Bays where one or more houseboats are moored and which area is zoned by Ordinance No. 630 for the mooring of houseboats either permanently or on a temporary basis.

Section 2: Houseboat Requirements. No person shall use or occupy or permit the use or occupancy of a houseboat for living quarters, either permanently or on a temporary basis, within the City of Sausalito, except when established in a specific location for which a Conditional Use Permit has been issued pursuant to the Zoning regulations of the City of Sausalito, and when such houseboat meets the following additional requirements:

(a) *Construction.* Every houseboat shall be inspected and approved by the Director of Public Works of the City of Sausalito, or the Sausalito Building Inspector, or any individual qualified to render such inspection and duly authorized by the City of Sausalito to do so for the problems of buoyance, windage, stability and structure, and for compliance with this ordinance.

(b) *Safety.* Every houseboat shall be supplied with life-saving equipment and extinguishers, access to circumference of the houseboat, and adequate means of egress.

(c) *Water Connection.* Every houseboat shall have a secure water connection above the waterline with an approved back-flow prevention device.

(d) *Electrical Connection.* Every houseboat shall have a permanent and adequate electrical connection.

(e) *Sewer.* Every houseboat shall be connected to a public sewer system with adequate vents, tanks and ejector devices. A.B.S. and P.V.C. may be used for drainage and vents. Should a public sewer not be available, then other devices acceptable to the Regional Water Quality Control Board may be used. Holding tanks designed and intended to accept all waste discharges from house-boats may be approved by the City of Sausalito in those instances where direct sanitary sewer connections cannot be accomplished.

(f) *Mooring.* Every houseboat shall maintain adequate lines, cleats and other necessary mooring equipment. This shall be inspected by the owner and / or operator of the marina or property upon which or within which such watercraft are located preceding the winter season.

(g) *Gangway [Secondary Walkway].* Every houseboat shall have a firm and substantial walkway extending from houseboat to mooring docks.

(h) *Construction Specifications.* All construction shall conform to specifications established by the City of Sausalito.

Section 3: Houseboat Permits. Any person desiring to maintain a houseboat within the City of Sausalito shall file with the City an application for a Certificate of Occupancy. Such Certificate of Occupancy shall not be issued unless the houseboat complies with the provisions set forth in Section 2, and the following requirements:

(a) Such craft shall be located in an appropriate zoning district.

(b) Payment of fees based upon the rates established by the Uniform Building Code.

Section 4: New Construction Permits. No person shall commence the construction, alteration or renovation of any houseboat within the City of Sausalito, or move a houseboat into the City of Sausalito, for use within the City of Sausalito, until he has first obtained from the Building Inspector of the City of Sausalito a permit authorizing such work. The fees for such permits shall be based upon the rates established by the Uniform Building Code. All and any work thereafter shall be accomplished in conformance with the requirements set forth in Section 2.

Section 5: Houseboat Marina Requirements. No person shall rent or hold out for rent any site or space for the establishment or location of a houseboat without having first secured a permit from the City to do so. The following requirements shall be satisfied before issuance of such permit:

(a) The owners and / or operators of any marina or water area within the City of Sausalito upon which any houseboat is proposed to be located shall furnish to the City of Sausalito the following information:

(1) The number of houseboats located or proposed to be located within the subject marina.

(2) A brief physical description of all such houseboats.

(3) The names of the legal owners and their addresses of all such houseboats.

(4) The location within the marinas of all such houseboats.

(5) Such information required by Section 5, 1 through 4 inclusive, shall further be provided to the City of Sausalito on an annual basis.

(b) *Garbage.* The owners and / or operators shall provide enclosed garbage receptacles in an accessible location for the use of houseboat occupants. No garbage, trash or refuse shall be dumped into the waters of San Francisco or Richardson Bays.

(c) *Parking.* The owners and / or operators shall provide off street parking in accordance with the parking standards set forth in the zoning regulations of the City of Sausalito.

(d) *Mooring.* The mooring plan of every marina should achieve the best in personal safety and aesthetics for its individual problems. All houseboats shall float at plus 5 feet above Mean Low Low Water unless, upon Conditional Use Permit review, a greater depth may be required should surrounding uses so demand and require.

(e) *Location.* No houseboat marina shall be established or developed except in compliance with all applicable zoning regulations.

(f) *Pump-Out Facility.* There shall be provided in each houseboat marina in which are located houseboats utilizing holding tanks a permanent holding tank pump-out facility or equivalent services which are operable and available for use at all times and which are capable of servicing all houseboats berthed, docked, or moored at said marina or anchorage area.

Section 6: Applicability. The provisions of this ordinance shall be applicable to all houseboats located within the City of Sausalito at the time of adoption of this ordinance as well as any houseboats which may be located within the City of Sausalito subsequent to the adoption of this ordinance.

Section 7: Violation. Any person convicted of violating the provisions of this ordinance shall be guilty of an infraction and upon conviction thereof shall be punished by a fine not to exceed One Hundred ($100.00) Dollars.

Section 8: This ordinance shall go into effect thirty days after the date of its adoption. Within fifteen days after the date of its adoption, this ordinance shall be posted in at least three public places in the City of Sausalito or published in a newspaper of general circulation printed and published in the County of Marin and circulated in the City of Sausalito.

"Light On the Water" being launched

*"Everything seems much closer here. All you
have to do is reach out the door and ask to
borrow some honey. Everybody knows each
other."* —Bob

"To live in a houseboat in Sausalito is like moving into a floating trailer park." —Alan

it's the same old dream
the houseboat nosed in at the riverbank
maybe a soft tree over to the left
trailing its long branches down to the water
or then again, maybe it's not a river at all
but the curve of a bay
anyway the houseboat, all snug & smug & sweet
and the back yard flowing by serenely
and maybe I'm just sitting there
smiling and drinking midnight coffee
looking out at the moon dancing on the waters
while the houseboat nods and bows
tipping her skirts to the stars

LENORE KANDEL

man
is a
born architect

Houseboat graffiti

"I keep thinking this place is for transients, but people always come back, it's such an easy place to live. I'm an old timer—been here for five years." —Doug

Stephen and Judy Siskind's schooner, "Isabela"

"Mud squatters is a little more apropos, sometimes literally." —Elizabeth

52   Leila in the galley of "The Bluebird."

GETTING THE GALLEY TOGETHER

People think of the place that food is prepared in as the kitchen, however when you live on a houseboat or sailboat the kitchen is called a *galley.* The galley is a moving kitchen, a special and important place. Anyone who has ever been to sea can tell you that the morale and efficiency of the crew depends a whole lot on a happy stomach. Being on the water actually stimulates your appetite. It's important to organize your galley so that food is easy to get to, and easy to prepare. The galley on a typical sailboat is small and cramped. This is good if you are on rough seas, as you can usually wedge yourself in while you are cooking; but basically it is pretty small, and not very convenient. On a sailboat you will get used to stretching, bending and reaching anyway. There's usually more space on a houseboat, especially if you have designed the interior yourself. Keep in mind that everything must be stored and secured in order to avert accidents on a rough or windy day. It is especially important that all knives and sharp objects be put in drawers or boxes where they won't come crashing down and cause injury.

GALLEY STOVES AND FUELS

There are many types of galley stoves available depending upon the kind of fuel and space available. The safest and very practical galley stove is coal or wood-burning. You can usually find driftwood to burn. For sure, space will have to be made to stow wood or charcoal. Maybe a group of houseboaters could purchase several cords of wood and make a community storage place on the pier or close by on shore. Many marinas will be hooked up to the local power company, and in these places any gas or electric stove can be connected. Anchoring out on a houseboat or living on a sailboat means existing independently from the local power companies. Alternates to wood burning stoves are kerosene, alcohol, and bottled gas fueled stoves. Be very careful handling these fuels. Alcohol is a bit more desirable than kerosene as it can be extinguished with water should it ignite. Bottled gas stoves require careful installation and handling. They must be used absolutely correctly. The gas is heavier than air—it can collect in the bilges and explode with tremendous force by ignition from even a tiny spark. Bottled gas tanks must be installed above deck with shut off valves in the supply line above deck and on the stove. The deck valves (outside) must be easily accessible by the cook and the stove must be lit and turned off immediately when not in use. Leave a note by the stove and porthole where the valves are to remind yourself to turn both valves off. These stoves are far more dangerous than stoves that burn solid fuel, (wood, coal, charcoal) or liquid fuel, (kerosene or alcohol). *NEVER, NEVER*, use gasoline as a cooking or heating fuel. It is extremely dangerous and a great hazard on the water. For more information on fuel, fire safety and stoves, write to:

> The National Fire Protection Association
> 60 Batterymarch Street
> Boston, Massachusetts

> The Yacht Safety Bureau
> 21 West Street
> New York, New York

They publish several pamphlets on marine equipment available on request.

Stoves should be tightly secured and should have metal rails around the top to prevent pots from falling or sliding around in rough weather. There are many companys that sell marine-approved stoves. Here's some to write to for more information and free brochures.

WOODBURNING

> The Franklin Stove Foundry
> Box 1156
> Portland, Maine

WOOD, COAL, STOVE OIL, KEROSENE and DEISEL (excellent quality marine products)

> Washington Stove Works
> P.O. Box 687
> Everett, Washington
> 98201

WOODBURNING HEATER

> Ashley Thermostatic Woodburning Heater Co.
> P.O. Box 730
> Sheffield, Alabama
> 35660
> (see reprint from Whole Earth Catalogue)

ALCOHOL and ELECTRIC

> The Princess Cook Stove
> The Princess Manufacturing Corp.
> 741 South Fremont Avenue
> Alhambra, California

A word about fire extinguishers: have at least two in the galley. Keep things that are flammable; paper towels, oven mitts, etc. away from the stove. Use water to put out wood or paper fires. Use flour, sand, or preferably special chemical fire extinguishers to put out grease, flammable liquids, and electrical fires. *NEVER, NEVER* use water on an electrical fire (instant electrocution). Always use a chemical fire extinguisher to put out an electrical fire. Check your extinguishers at least once a year to make sure they are filled and functioning properly.

STOWING FOOD

Food is affected differently near ocean water. Everything should be put in waterproof containers to keep it dry and free from fungus and mildew. Gallon size plastic containers with screw-on lids, the kind that ketchup and mayonnnaise come in, are really handy for storing large amounts of dry goods and dried fruits. Several pounds of flour, sugar, oats or raisins (etc.) will fit into one of these. I found a local café that will save their empties for me rather than throw them out. Special dehumidifying cans and five-gallon plastic containers with lids and handles can be found at most army-navy surplus stores, and these are particularly good for storing bulky things, like potatoes and onions. All dry package goods should be put in plastic baggies and tied shut to keep the moisture out. Also, if you are tied to a pier you will want to make sure that everything edible is mouse proof. Put anything a mouse would go after in metal bread boxes or large tins with covers. I left some packaged snacks unwrapped and on a shelf in the galley overnight. By

morning every crumb had been eaten and a good deal of the cardboard packaging too! If you like cats, why not consider adopting some. They think mice are very tasty, and are great company at sea and on land.

Goods not properly stored will attract cockroaches and weevils. Always check your dry goods when you purchase them to make sure there are no weevils. One remedy for cockroaches is to mix borax and sugar together and put it in areas they are likely to infest. I don't like these little beasties in my galley and I do everything possible to avoid them. Remember, the more aggressive you are towards cockroaches, the less likely they are to stay around.

FRUITS, VEGETABLES AND MEATS

Dried fruits can be kept drier by rolling them in cornstarch before storing them. This process does not affect their taste and keeps them longer. If you have a refrigerator you will be able to keep meat, fish and fresh foods for quite awhile. If you don't have a refrigerator try a Coleman ice-box instead. Purchase a big block of ice to keep things chilled. The ice lasts about four days. Smoked meats and fish last longest. You can dry and smoke your fish or meat by slicing it very thin and placing it in a slightly warm oven for three or four hours. A wood burning stove would make the smoking a lot easier, but a simple hibachi will do. Most vegetables will keep for a week or more. For leafy veges, peel off the outer wilted leaves, the ones inside will still be fresh and usable. Most fruits will keep a week or more. Apples, stored in a dark place and individually wrapped will keep up to a month.

Stores that sell outdoor equipment for backpackers often carry many interesting and unique freeze dried meals, beverages and desserts. Two popular brands are *Mountain House* and *Tea Kettle*. Many items are available in bulk, they are all tasty and easy to prepare . . . even far out delicious treats like ice cream shakes, strawberries and peaches and chocolate cream pie! (Yummy) These foods are easy to store, take little space, and come in individually wrapped portions sealed in heavy foil packages. For more information write to:

Oregon Freeze Dry Foods, Inc.
P.O. Box 1048
Albany, Oregon 97321

". . . The sourdough stuff keeps rising and bubbling and falling as the temperature in the coldbox changes." —Judy

HOUSEBOAT SOUP AND OTHER RECIPES

The following is a letter from a friend about cooking and eating on board: "Thoroughly stimulated after an evening of candelit dining pleasure, quiet reading in a comfortable little main cabin seems altogether appropriate. When living toasty-warm below on rainy, windy nights, sipping mulled wine and reading aloud escapades of ships and men, it is easy to visualize the howling gales and electrical thunderstorms Chichester, Slocum and other mariners experienced while circumnavigating this earthly sphere. And, so it goes, living on board a sailboat expresses the simpleness of a Walden's Pond.

"Boat-living is an old fashioned and unfortunately dying form of relaxation and country-life. In a cosmopolitan area simplicity and peace of this sort can only be found near water, the closest sensitivity of nature left in citified areas after the land has been consumed with industry and suburbia.

"Separate and apart from the escapism and aesthetic factors, an education in life, nature and sea emerges. But, when referring to the 'simpleness' of this form of living, it must be remembered that it is in some ways more difficult, and unique complications such as condensation, cooking and lack of storage create problems of a different nature from life in a P.G.&E.-oriented apartment.

"It is really fun to find little nooks and crannies, or to build dish racks and other small storage structures out of coca-cola cartons or cigar boxes or whatever to form-fit into the boat's design. It is a non-furniture existence and getting rid of cumbersome furniture, extra clothing . . . reveals how few possessions and what a small amount of space men and women actually require to live comfortably. Throwing away old material attachments also furnishes a major tension release, and a new sense of freedom develops.

"Cooking on board can be as imaginative and delicious as those meals prepared in a gourmet kitchen of a large home. The most practical combinations are soups and casseroles because of the minimal number of dishes and pans involved. Most boats, whether house or sail, have no hot water for washing dishes. Water has to be heated, which creates condensation problems with steam floating through the air, so it is preferable to closely limit dishwashing periods. So, developing new chowders and stews adds to the education of boat-living. Also, since most houseboats and sailboats have little refrigeration, storing fresh vegetables, eggs, and meat, dairy products is difficult. Meals should be prepared so thereare no left-overs that require storing. Sometimes a stew is good as it can sit on the top of the stove and just be re-heated each day. While fresh foods are always best, some canned goods can be kept around for emergency. When fresh meat and milk products are unavailable, a simple wine sauce from canned or bottled products can spiff up even the dullest dish.

WINE SAUCE: 1 small can evaporated milk
2 T. butter (fresh or canned)
1 boullion cube
1 / 4 c. water
1 / 2 - 1 c. Wine

"Canned goods tend to rust very quickly. Condensation will usually cause labels to start sliding off after only a few weeks. In addition to creating a can-identification problem, if the cans are kept in an ice chest, it could also cause a drain-clogging problem. The best cure so far seems to be a coating of non-toxic paint for rust prevention and then painting symbols of identification or colorful pictures on the sides." —Nancy May

A pressure cooker would be a most useful item in your galley. It will cut your cooking time in half. Be sure when pressure cooking to read the instructions on the pressure cooker and reduce the pressure instantly when the food is done. Use teflon pots and pans. Cast iron will rust.

Houseboat Soup with Seaweed

Soak seaweed in water, about 10 minutes. Chop vegetables—anything really—garlic, onions, scallions, carrots, broccoli, celery, mushrooms, water chestnuts; the more exotic the better. Cook vegetables in water, add seaweed with or without its own water depending on how strong you want it. I always add it. Add Tamari and herbs to taste, usually a couple of tablespoons. Heat it up well and let it simmer, add several well-beaten eggs, stir, and serve hot. Garnish with a chunk of cheese or croutons.

Fish Chowders

2 - 3 lbs. of fish
2 onions - chopped
2 - 4 potatoes - cubed
2 carrots sliced thin
1 / 2 lb. salt pork
1 quart milk (use powdered milk if fresh is not available)
Salt and pepper to taste
Add herbs and seasonings as desired.
Add enough water to cover fish - allow it to cook 10 - 15 minutes. Add vegetables, salt pork and seasoning. Simmer till tender, add butter if desired and serve.

The Best Whole Wheat Bread

Add a little less than 1 tablespoon active dry yeast to 1 cup lukewarm water and let dissolve. Combine:
   4 cups whole wheat flour
   little more than 1 / 2 cup raw sugar or honey
   little more than 1 teaspoon salt
   4 tablespoons wheatgerm
Mix yeast and water. You may have to add 1 / 2 to 1 cup more water depending on the weather. The dough should be a rather sticky consistency. Let rise to about 1 / 2 volume, then place in a greased and floured bread pan or coffee tin. Let rise again to top of pan. Place in 350 oven 45 minutes to 1 hour.

Cowboy Coffee

Put the coffee in the bottom of the pot and add the water. Bring to a boil and turn off flame. Let it stand for a few minutes and then add a little cool water. Wait till the coffee grounds settle to the bottom and then pour. This method is excellent for brewing tea too. Add the tea leaves after the water boils. Let the tea leaves steep for 3 - 5 minutes. Pour.

Fried Tofu (Soybean Curd)

Slice Tofu into 1" slices and dip in a mixture of wheatgerm and herbs. A batter may be made of eggs, wheat germ, brewer's yeast and a little water or milk. Fry in hot oil; I use Safflower oil. Tamari may be used for seasoning. For special flavor use some fresh grated ginger.

Beansprouts

There are several commercial bean sprouters available that will sprout all the sprouts you can eat. Check at your local health food store. It is easy to make a homemade sprouter with a glass jar and some cheesecloth and rubberbands. Put the beans in the jar and let them soak overnight. Rinse them in the morning, cover the jar with the cheesecloth, turn upside down and let drain. Let sit upside down and rinse once everyday until sprouted.

To Bake Bread or Cakes in Coffee Cans:

Knead dough on a flat surface and grease cans. Fill with dough and let rise if recipe is a yeast dough. Bake in oven. When through remove bread from cans and slice.

German Pancake

No. 8 skillet
5 - 7 or more eggs

Proportions are:
   1 egg
   1 ounce flour   (2 eggs - 2 ozs. flour and 2 ozs. milk, etc.)
   1 ounce milk
   pinch of salt
Beat ingredients with beater until there are bubbles in the mixture. Warm skillet with 2 - 4 tablespoons of butter, pour in mixture and place in 425 oven for 15 - 25 minutes.

Potato Soup (A very thick soup)

6 - 8 or more large potatoes
Slice potatoes in half or quarters. Cover with water and let boil. Add 1 / 4 cube of butter or margarine. Salt and Pepper to taste. Add 3 or more thick slices of ham. Cook for an hour and serve hot.

"Things here are slow. Living on the water gives you a stretched-out time quality. When you live with all the elements, your time-space thing gets warped." —Bruce

MARINE FIRE EXTINGUISHERS

There are three kinds of marine fire extinguishers.

1. *CO2 - Carbon Dioxide* - This type is for closed areas, it is not harmful to food, clothing, mechanical or electrical equipment.

2. *Dry Chemical* - This type is for open and closed areas. It is effective on flammable liquid and electrical fires. It is not harmful to clothing.

3. *Foam* - This is for open and closed areas. It is NOT RECOMMENDED for electrical fires as the foam may conduct electricity from the fire to the operator.

Flammable liquids are gasoline, kerosene, oil, and stove alcohol. CO_2 extinguishers need to be recharged whenever there is a weight loss of 10 or more. Dry chemical extinguishers should be serviced annually if they have an indicating device and semi-annually if there is no indicating device on the tank. Foam extinguishers should be discharged and recharged annually if they have an indicating device and semi-annually if there is no indicating device on the tank. Foam extinguishers should be discharged and recharged annually.

Never use water to put out an electrical fire as it conducts electricity. Never use water on gasoline or oil fires, these fuels will float and the water may actually spread the fire.

Keep all fire extinguishers in easily accessible places, so in an emergency you can get to them fast.

FRESH WATER

You will need plenty of fresh water to drink and cook with. Even though the shore and stores may be relatively close by, when you are anchored out you will still need bottled water for drinking. Springwater may be purchased in gallon jugs and stowed away, if you have a storage tank and space, five-gallon size bottles are available from most water companies. The amount of fresh water to keep on board will vary according to the number of people there are, and how far away it is to replenish your supply, but generally you should allow for at least eight glasses of water a day for each person.

It is a good idea to wash off objects that fall into salt water, as the salt will corrode metal and other materials.

FRESH WATER FROM SALT WATER

It is possible to make a limited amount of fresh water from salt water, or any brackish water, by using a device known as a solar still. It is a good device on a small boat with little space for water storage, on a houseboat, anchored out, or anywhere you would desire to make fresh water. It could be designed right into the hull as a permanent source for fresh water. Basically, it requires sunshine, an insulated box, a piece of glass, sponge or dark rocks, and some small hoses. It is not difficult to construct one from any box. However, a foam box, like the kind used for some portable ice chests and picnic boxes is best because it provides good insulation and keeps the seawater at an even temperature that helps to prevent the growth of algae. Algae cannot grow if the temperature is over 110 degrees. Foam is so well insulated that one sunny day kills the algae.

A solar still will produce up to a half gallon of fresh water daily from two and one half gallons seawater. Basically it is a box with a liner that won't leak, like black polyethelene. You could use rocks in the bottom, or special acrylic laytex black paint, or (preferable) if you are on the water and moving about a lot a dark sponge placed in the bottom of the box, will absorb the sea water and keep it from sloshing around. On top of the box is a sloped piece of glass; the box is sealed with black tape and holes are made to take in seawater and for the fresh water to run out of as it condenses on the underside of the glass and runs down. You must use glass because moisture will not run down plastic or plexiglass. It will only bead and drip back into the solar still. After you add the seawater the solar still is placed in sunlight and as the rays heat it, the water will condense on the underside of the glass and run out into the collection receptacle. The box should have short hoses attached to the opening where you add seawater, and leading to the fresh water collection gutter and into the collection container.

I went to the University of California Seawater Conversion Laboratory, at Richmond, California, where I spoke with J.O. Hensley (Sandy) who has co-invented, with Paul Young, a portable, solar still, to be used primarily by people with small boats, sailboats, houseboats, and limited space. They have patented a small unit, (patent no. 365517) which will produce up to 1 / 2 gallon fresh water per day. A family of four could exist on the fresh water produced from four of these units. Hensley and Young hope to market these stills and have them available to the public very soon.

Hensley and Young also have designed a solar still unit which folds up for storage when not in use. It will float, so if it went overboard you could retrieve it, and if you went overboard you could use it as a survival flotation device. Hensley said these units could even be used in the desert to make fresh water from poisonous water or cactus and other vegetation. The poison cannot be carried in the vapor as it condenses on the underside of the glass. For more information write to:

Mr. J.O. Hensley
c / o Seawater Conversion Laboratory
University of California, Richmond Field Station
1301 South 45th Street
Richmond, California

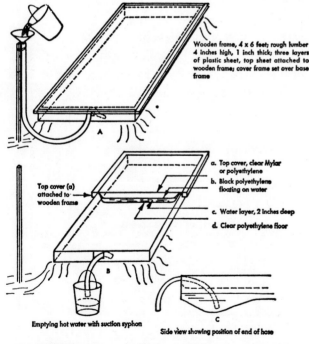

Wooden frame, 4 x 6 feet; rough lumber 4 inches high, 1 inch thick; three layers of plastic sheet, top sheet attached to wooden frame; cover frame set over base frame

Top cover (a) attached to wooden frame

a. Top cover, clear Mylar or polyethylene
b. Black polyethylene floating on water
c. Water layer, 2 inches deep
d. Clear polyethylene floor

Emptying hot water with suction syphon

Side view showing position of end of hose

29. Inexpensive solar water heater. A. Filling with cold water. B. Emptying hot water with suction syphon. C. Side view, showing position of end of hose.

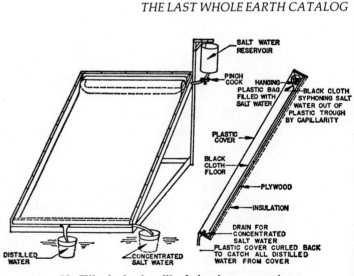

SALT WATER RESERVOIR

PINCH COCK

PLASTIC BAG FILLED WITH SALT WATER

HANGING

BLACK CLOTH SYPHONING SALT WATER OUT OF PLASTIC TROUGH BY CAPILLARITY

PLASTIC COVER

BLACK CLOTH FLOOR

PLYWOOD

INSULATION

DRAIN FOR CONCENTRATED SALT WATER

PLASTIC COVER CURLED BACK TO CATCH ALL DISTILLED WATER FROM COVER

DISTILLED WATER

CONCENTRATED SALT WATER

32. Tilted plastic still of simple construction.

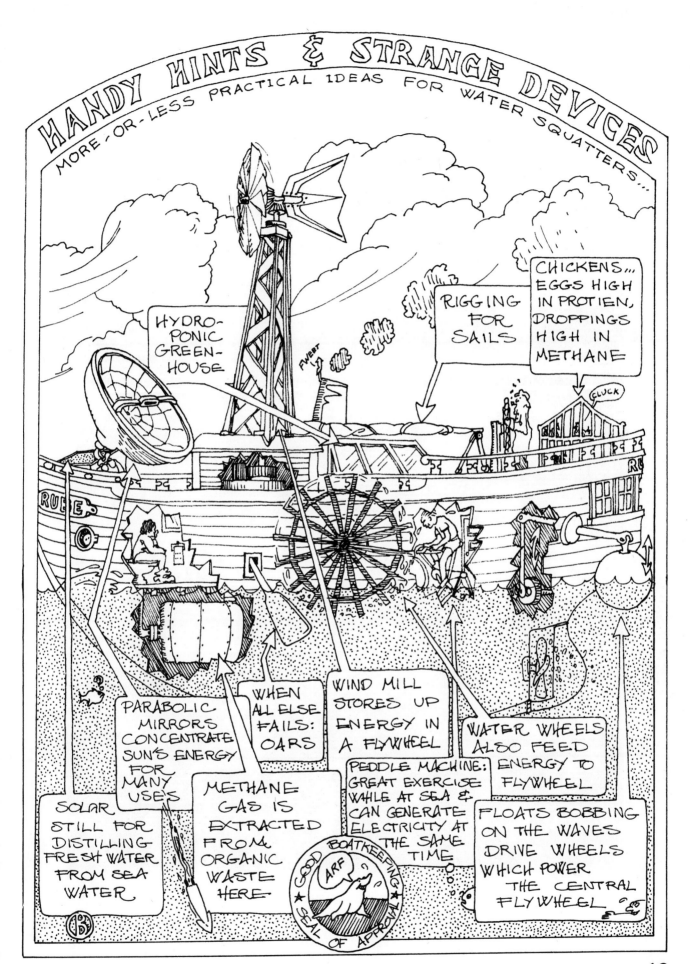

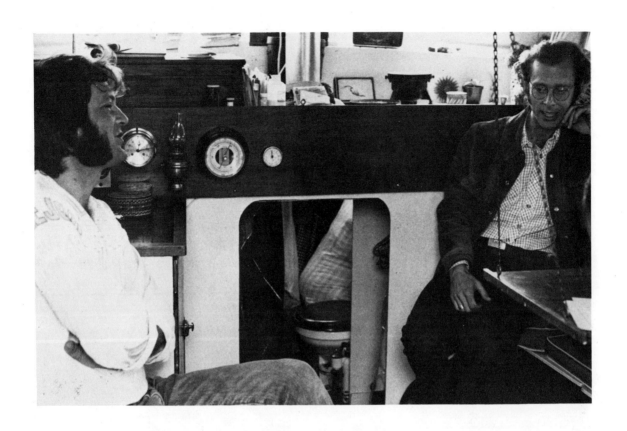

Captain Jerry Corbitt and R.P. St. John on "The Bluebird."

SANITATION

Most berths are fairly inexpensive, and for about $50 per month you can tie up your boat. Most docks include utilities, water, gas and electricity and a hook-up to the sewage system if there is one. Raw sewage and garbage in the water is a problem and a health menace. Cleanliness of the water and shore is the responsibility of the people who live on it and use it.

There are alternatives to the marine head which flushes raw sewage into the water. Some of these are the Jerry John, Monomatic Toilet and Porta-Potty, available at most sporting goods or marine supply stores.

Try to not pollute the water. Use biodegradable soap and other products that declare on the label they are not harmful to the environment.

"The cheapest and easiest way for me is to build a box with a toilet seat on it and take it to shore." —Peter

MOVING YOUR HOUSEBOAT

Tugboats assist vessels to and from the docks to other vessels, and to the shipyards to be worked on. Tugboats usually will only move something that is seaworthy, not something that may sink. A tug cannot put a line on a houseboat in the mud, but if your houseboat is afloat and seaworthy, most tugs will tow your boat. The cost will depend on the job, the hourly rate for a tugboat is usually between $75 - $150.

"When I lived on the bay I was studying astrology really heavy. I was impressed by my boat rising six feet with the tides. It helped me understand the gravity of the planets." —Patty

GARDENS

Gardening is possible on a houseboat, but with an entirely different set of problems. You aren't as aware of the seasons changing as you are on land. You've got to see it happen and participate, i.e., Plants and Gardens. All plants, flowers, vegetables and trees must be grown in boxes of dirt. You must guard your plants from salt, and repot them often. Plants kept in boxes should be particularly hardy. They feel the weather more because everything is reflected off the water. It's a good idea to keep your garden boxes covered with chicken wire in order to keep out dogs, cats, and birds. Succulents grow very well near the water; also ivy, ferns, peas, beans and herbs.

SEATTLE

Seattle has a very organized houseboat community. Most of the moorings are locked and you must have a key to the gate to get onto the dock. The marinas have a sewage system and no waste goes into the water. The houseboats are docked close to each other in orderly rows, closer than most developments on land, yet clanking and rocking with the water.

Each houseboat has its own garbage can on shore that is picked up regularly by the trash man. Mail boxes too are on shore, with addresses as on residential streets. The Seattle houseboats must conform to city code and are inspected occasionally. Most of them are built from new materials in contrast to Sausalito, for example, where so many are freely constructed from recycled boats, houses and anything else that can be made to work.

"A person that's going to live on water is a slightly unusual person to begin with." —Capt. Jerry Corbitt of the Royal Marshall Navy

"We've all been healthier living on the water."
—Bess

WIND GENERATOR

I saw a ferro-cement sailboat with a small windmill. The windmill runs a generator that lights a 100-watt bulb. The blade was about 4 feet across, was mounted 7 feet high and could be detached.

DOMES - SKYVENTS

There are many commercial domes, plastic bubbles and skyvents available to install into your houseboat for more light. One designed especially for marine use is the Sudbury Sky Vent.

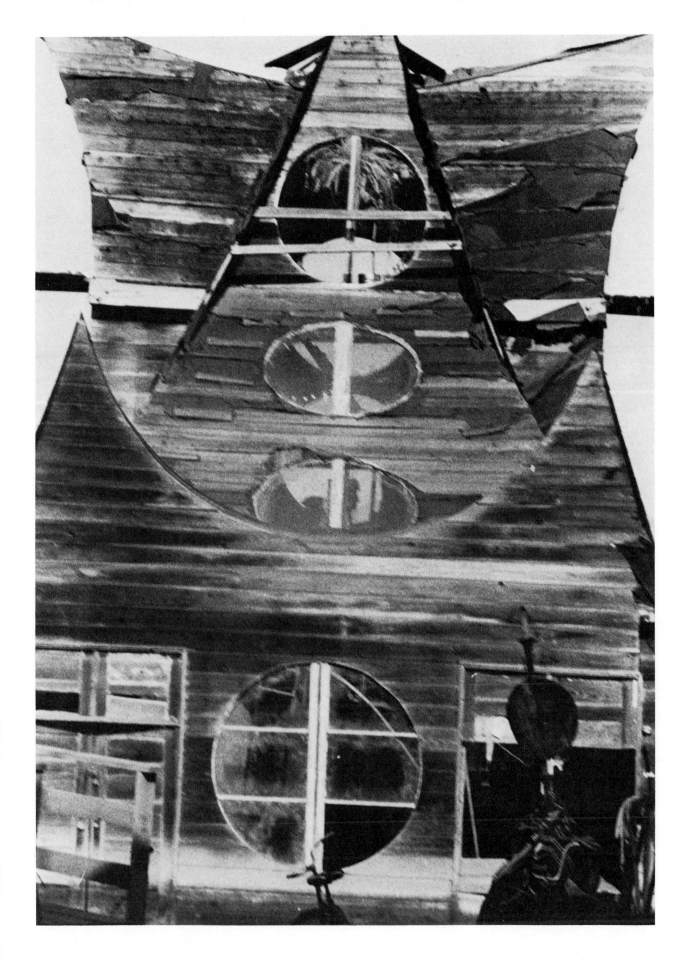

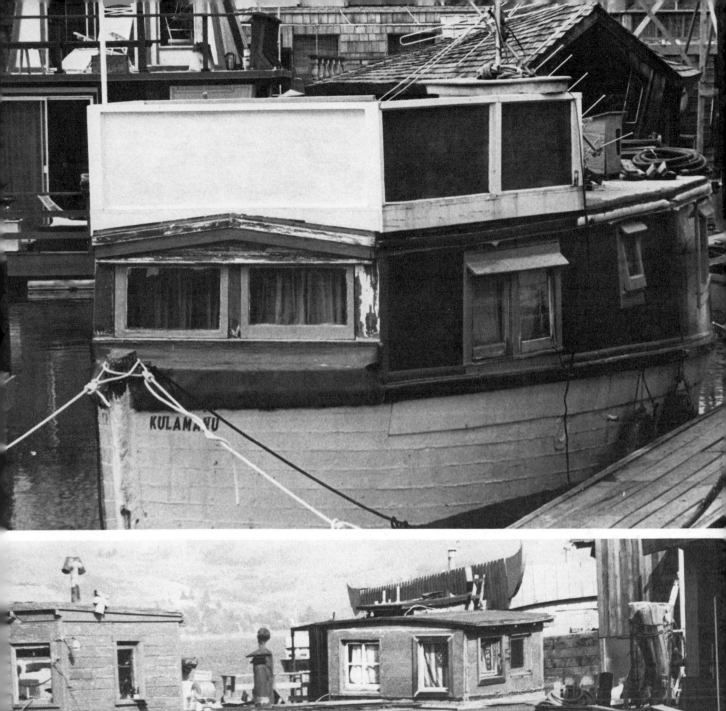

"It's unconventional for people to act unconventional. People living on the water are together in a funny kind of way. Many say that the tides do affect them." —Patty

A houseboat friend.

Basic Utensils and other Handy Items.

Flour sifter
Measuring spoons
Measuring cups
Assorted unbreakable bowls
Egg Beater
Wooden Spoons
at least 2 sharp knives
Spatula
Roasting Pan or Casserole (Teflon)
Can Openers (both kinds)
Tongs
Tin foil
Cheesecloth
Jar for beansprouts
Cookie sheet
Muffin tin and muffin tin papers
Cake pan
Dishtowels
Cloth napkins
Rubber gloves
Nylon tuffies for dishwashing
    (steel wool will rust)
Plastic dish pan
Biodegradable soap
Baggies
Paper Towels

Assorted Spices and Herbs for Seasonings

Allspice
Basil
Black Pepper
Bay Leaves
Cardammon Seeds
Cayenne
Coriander
Chili Powder
Cinnamon
Cloves
Curry
Cumin
Dill
Ginger
Garlic Powder
Marjoram
Mint
Mustard Powder
Paprika
Nutmeg
Oregano
Parsley
Onion Powder
Rosemary
Saffron
Sage
Sea Salt
Tarragon
Thyme
Vanilla Bean and extract
Almond extract
Vegesal
Tamari (soybean sauce)

"The Redlegs"—The official houseboat community band.

CHILDREN ABOARD

There are many exciting things for children to discover around the water. Sea shells and driftwood provide material for home-made windchimes and jewelry. Sculpture made from driftwood and things washed up on the beach is fun to glue and nail together. How about making an abacus from sea shells? Sand can be used to make sandpaper by covering a piece of heavy paper with glue and sprinkling fine sand over it. Try making quills from seagull feathers. Cut off the tops of the feathers and tie the quills into bundles. Place the bundles upright in boiling water with 2 tablespoons of Alum. Boil the quills until they are clear and then set them in the sun to dry. The more alum you use, the stiffer the quills will be.

Most marinas allow children of any age to live on a houseboat or boat, though some marinas have age restrictions. There are very few piers that don't allow children.

Jessica Corbitt on "The Bluebird"

ATTENTION
DOG OWNERS
DOG RULES
1. No more NEW DOGS allowed
2. No dogs allowed in rental units
3. No visiting dogs allowed on docks
4. Dogs are not allowed to run loose

Non-Compliance of these rules will result in EVICTION.
KAPAS YACHT HARBOR

NO Children under age 15 allowed to LIVE on BOATS or HOUSEBOATS

Marsha and some friends.

Nicole and daughter.

101

ANIMALS

Cats are usually welcome as they keep the mouse population down. Dogs may or may not be allowed. At some docks there is a monthly fee for each animal you keep, the money goes to pay someone to keep the piers clean. Dogs and cats should be vaccinated yearly for distemper and rabies. Use dramamine to keep your pets from motion sickness until they get used to the movement of the water. Animals usually adjust rapidly to living on a houseboat.

Jerry and Fat Albert

"You have to ration drinking and cooking water because you have to row it out to the boat."

Fat Albert

Dhyana and Larry and the cat.

MARY

"You watch the weather more. You watch the winds and the barometer, and you can pretty much tell what's going to happen." —Jerry

Sacramento River Delta

Stanley trying to keep afloat.

SACRAMENTO RIVER DELTA

They say if you stretched the Delta waterways and levee roads into a straight line, they would reach New York. It's a fascinating region of asparagus farms, antique hamlets, swampy islands and drawbridges. The best way to explore this region, an hour's drive from San Francisco, is to rent a houseboat with several people for as little as $10 per person, and float down the fingering waterways. Three types of houseboats may be rented: Delta Marina offers the "picnic barge," for day use only; then there's the catamaran houseboat (or pontoon hulls), stable and easy for beginners to navigate with an average speed of 6-8 mph; and the cruiser hull, powered by a single or twin inboard engine, recommended for experienced boaters planning a long cruise. Both the pontoon and cruiser vary from 30-50 feet and come with stove, refrigerator, beds, closets and a bathroom. They rent from $100-$200 a weekend, $315-$450 per week in the summer season; from $225-$350 a week in the off season. Reservations must be made months in advance. The rental people will instruct you in navigation and docking, though you are expected to know boating regulations. Read *"ABC's of California Boating Laws"* or *"Safe Boating on the Sacramento River,"* from the Department of Navigation and Ocean Development.

There are good maps of the Delta: *"Weekend Outdoor Map,"* available at marinas and bait stores, and *"Delta Region Map,"* (write Delta Marina Yacht Harbor, 100 Marina Drive, Rio Vista—send $1 plus 25c postage) which shows bridges clearance (houseboats need 11 ft.), water depth and all resort and boat harbors in the Delta.

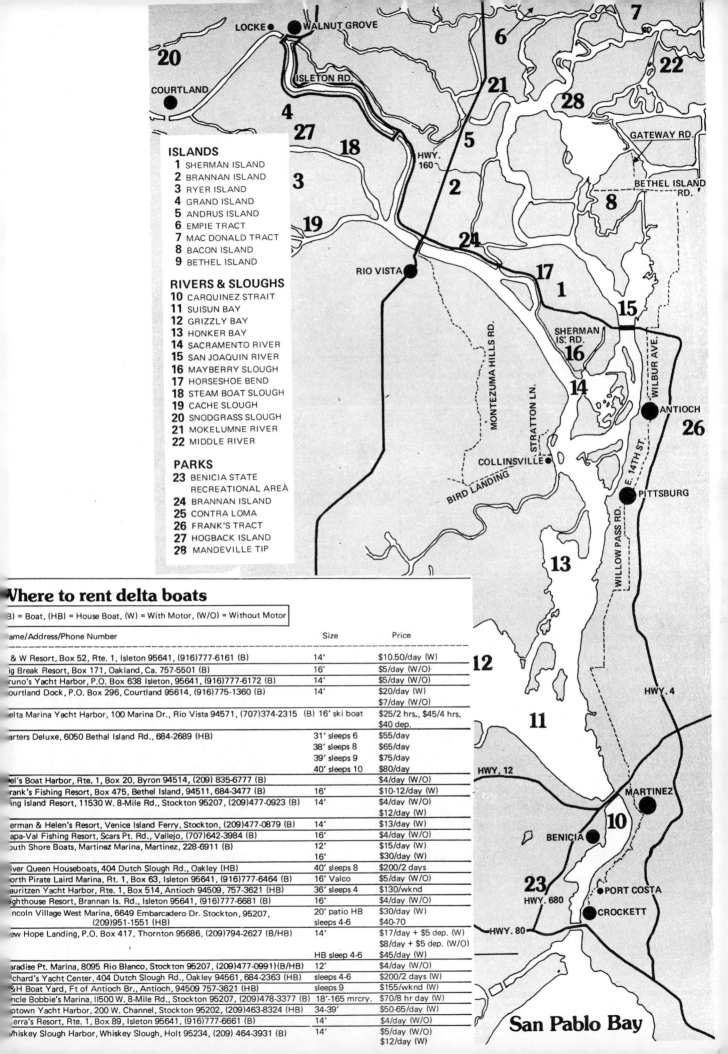

ISLANDS
1. SHERMAN ISLAND
2. BRANNAN ISLAND
3. RYER ISLAND
4. GRAND ISLAND
5. ANDRUS ISLAND
6. EMPIE TRACT
7. MAC DONALD TRACT
8. BACON ISLAND
9. BETHEL ISLAND

RIVERS & SLOUGHS
10. CARQUINEZ STRAIT
11. SUISUN BAY
12. GRIZZLY BAY
13. HONKER BAY
14. SACRAMENTO RIVER
15. SAN JOAQUIN RIVER
16. MAYBERRY SLOUGH
17. HORSESHOE BEND
18. STEAM BOAT SLOUGH
19. CACHE SLOUGH
20. SNODGRASS SLOUGH
21. MOKELUMNE RIVER
22. MIDDLE RIVER

PARKS
23. BENICIA STATE RECREATIONAL AREA
24. BRANNAN ISLAND
25. CONTRA LOMA
26. FRANK'S TRACT
27. HOGBACK ISLAND
28. MANDEVILLE TIP

Where to rent delta boats

(B) = Boat, (HB) = House Boat, (W) = With Motor, (W/O) = Without Motor

Name/Address/Phone Number	Size	Price
B & W Resort, Box 52, Rte. 1, Isleton 95641, (916)777-6161 (B)	14'	$10.50/day (W)
Big Break Resort, Box 171, Oakland, Ca. 757-5501 (B)	16'	$5/day (W/O)
Bruno's Yacht Harbor, P.O. Box 638 Isleton, 95641, (916)777-6172 (B)	14'	$5/day (W/O)
Courtland Dock, P.O. Box 296, Courtland 95614, (916)775-1360 (B)	14'	$20/day (W) $7/day (W/O)
Delta Marina Yacht Harbor, 100 Marina Dr., Rio Vista 94571, (707)374-2315 (B)	16' ski boat	$25/2 hrs., $45/4 hrs. $40 dep.
Charters Deluxe, 6050 Bethal Island Rd., 684-2689 (HB)	31' sleeps 6	$55/day
	38' sleeps 8	$65/day
	39' sleeps 9	$75/day
	40' sleeps 10	$80/day
Del's Boat Harbor, Rte. 1, Box 20, Byron 94514, (209) 835-6777 (B)		$4/day (W/O)
Frank's Fishing Resort, Box 475, Bethel Island, 94511, 684-3477 (B)	16'	$10-12/day (W)
King Island Resort, 11530 W. 8-Mile Rd., Stockton 95207, (209)477-0923 (B)	14'	$4/day (W) $12/day (W)
Herman & Helen's Resort, Venice Island Ferry, Stockton, (209)477-0879 (B)	14'	$13/day (W)
Napa-Val Fishing Resort, Scars Pt. Rd., Vallejo, (707)642-3984 (B)	16'	$4/day (W/O)
South Shore Boats, Martinez Marina, Martinez, 228-6911 (B)	12'	$15/day (W)
	16'	$30/day (W)
River Queen Houseboats, 404 Dutch Slough Rd., Oakley (HB)	40' sleeps 8	$200/2 days
North Pirate Laird Marina, Rt. 1, Box 63, Isleton 95641, (916)777-6464 (B)	16' Valco	$5/day (W/O)
Mauritzen Yacht Harbor, Rte. 1, Box 514, Antioch 94509, 757-3621 (HB)	36' sleeps 4	$130/wknd
Lighthouse Resort, Brannan Is. Rd., Isleton 95641, (916)777-6681 (B)	16'	$4/day (W)
Lincoln Village West Marina, 6649 Embarcadero Dr. Stockton, 95207, (209)951-1551 (HB)	20' patio HB sleeps 4-6	$30/day (W) $40-70
New Hope Landing, P.O. Box 417, Thornton 95686, (209)794-2627 (B/HB)	14'	$17/day + $5 dep. (W) $8/day + $5 dep. (W/O)
	HB sleep 4-6	$45/day (W)
Paradise Pt. Marina, 8095 Rio Blanco, Stockton 95207, (209)477-0991 (B/HB)	12'	$4/day (W/O)
Richard's Yacht Center, 404 Dutch Slough Rd., Oakley 94561, 684-2363 (HB)	sleeps 4-6	$200/2 days (W)
J&H Boat Yard, Ft of Antioch Br., Antioch, 94509 757-3621 (HB)	sleeps 9	$155/wknd (W)
Uncle Bobbie's Marina, 11500 W. 8-Mile Rd., Stockton 95207, (209)478-3377 (B)	18'-165 mrcry.	$70/8 hr day (W)
Uptown Yacht Harbor, 200 W. Channel, Stockton 95202, (209)463-8324 (HB)	34-39'	$50-65/day (W)
Sierra's Resort, Rte. 1, Box 89, Isleton 95641, (916)777-6661 (B)	14'	$4/day (W/O)
Whiskey Slough Harbor, Whiskey Slough, Holt 95234, (209) 464-3931 (B)	14'	$5/day (W/O) $12/day (W)

San Pablo Bay

ELSEWHERE IN AMERICA

—New York

"A real sense of small town," is how the dockmaster characterizes a flotilla of houseboats anchored in the Hudson River by the shores of Manhattan. They—an actress, advertising executives, professional photographers, families with children—don't advertise their existence. They feel they're out of the rat race and pay $16-a-foot for their houseboats during the winter, and $21-a-foot the rest of the year. The reality of small town life is quickly apparent. Unlike huge impersonal apartment houses, boaters soon know their neighbors. Cooperation is a way of life. The boat shed serves as post office and unofficial city hall. They say it takes about a week to get acclimated to rocking.

—Corona, S.D.

Back in South Dakota, a cattle rancher, stung by a falling cattle market, decided to get away with his family. He built himself a 70-foot houseboat constructed from fiberglassed 2-by-6 planks and topped by a wheel-house. He launched it on the Missouri River at Sioux City in the spring, and headed for New Orleans, with plans to head up the west coast to Alaska, working along the way as a welder.

—Sausalito, Ca.

Here, where it has a center, the old ferryboat "Vallejo", home of the late painter, Varda, lives Marion Saltman, friend and spiritual playmate of the late Alan Watts, where she teaches groups of adults to play, be young and resilient. "Pleasure," she says, "is more difficult to explain than pain, particularly with grown-ups."

HOUSEBOATS IN OTHER LANDS

Amsterdam

Hong Kong

Bangkok

Kashmir

VIEW FROM A HOUSEBOAT IN BENARES, INDIA

Inside our houseboat, white and clean, adorned only with two large paintings under glass, of Gods and their consorts, beatific cows and peacocks in cool, moonlit jungles; and on the white wooden wall by the ceiling, as a border, a tiny mural of Krishna happily riding a crocodile across the holy Ganges river (known as "the Ganga," the source of all life, the beginning and end to every Indian). This, and most of the other houseboats all moored at the watery entrances of Maharajas' palaces or temples—there are 30,000 built for the worship of Lord Shiva and Parvati, Ganesha, and the more ancient Ram, the God of blue with bow and arrow shooting souls to Heaven—are there for devotees at sunrise to float along the river in worship, singing soft and melodious songs to the many thousand Gods and Goddesses in the Hindu pantheon and chanting mantras to the river itself, the literal source of life rushing down a thousand miles from the melting snows of the Himalayas and here flowing swiftly, yet still in its vastness—500 feet in depth and more than a mile wide. We drank from the depths where the waters are most pure and bathed each day on the steps of a little temple to Shiva . . . wreaths of marigolds and other flowers floating serenely by on the many currents of the river . . . ancient boats too, with sails the colors of the enormous red sphere of the rising sun across the river, dazzling the river with all shades of pinks, rosy hues, peach, topaz and lavenders; and, now and then bobbing silently along the river an amethyst-colored corpse of a holy man or baby (the only ones privileged enough to be slipped into the river at death because they are the closest to the source). Most people require purification by fire, their ashes offered to the Ganga, powdered by the winds. Enormous blue black ravens, green parrots and blond Gibbon monkeys live all along the steps of the crumbling magnificence of architecture, multi-dimensional, all palaces and temples, silk weaving looms in cool white chalk rooms aglow with the vivid color of the silk; universities, monasteries, on the crescent moon-shaped steps of stone descending three hundred feet into the river; the river wrapping round the stone into the narrow streets that, at times, become enormous perfect stairs built for Gods.

Exquisitely peaceful and deep clear silence on the boat all night except for the sudden pleasant sound of heavy cymbals, tiny finger cymbals, and the singing chants of those meditating through the night. Then the silence again, the river slipping softly beneath the wooden floor. Through your body come soothing currents, harmonizing and purifying in sleep each night. In the day, with all green shutters open for the sun, fresh breeze, blue sky and converse with a fifteen foot black porpoise who was always near our boat day and night for two months . . . his joyous presence flowing soothing in the Tao and friendly, teaching us and protecting too.

Macao

BACK HOME AGAIN

"You have the feeling of being totally exposed."
—Judy

MISCELLANEOUS INFORMATION

Season pots and frypans so they won't rust on the water. Coat them lightly with oil.

Keep a portable washtub and washboard for doing laundry on board.

Rope, Knots and Splices

Nylon rope is preferable to hemp rope because the saltwater won't eat away at it. No matter which rope you prefer, in order to tie your houseboat to the pier you will need to know some simple knots and splices. There are many good references, some of these are:

    The Ashley Book of Knots - Clifford Ashley

    Knots and Splices- P.W. Blandford

    Handbook of Knots - Raoul Graumont

All of these books are clearly illustrated and easy to understand.

Health Hints and Water Safety

It's a good idea to know a little basic first aid and water safety. Children and adults should learn survival swimming and rescue breathing techniques. Young children should wear life-preservers while playing on the docks and elsewhere in the harbor area. There is always a danger of drowning. Even experienced swimmers have been known to panic when accidentally submerged. The American National Red Cross offers free or low cost courses in swimming and first aid. If there is no Red Cross in your area, try the YMCA or YWCA.

There are many good first aid books available for the layman. In particular the American National Red Cross first aid pamphlet, and the *Ship Captain's Medical Guide.*

Here are some places to write to for information about various houseboat kits.

Glen-L Marine Designs
9152 Rosecrans
Bellflower, California 90706

Luger Industries, Inc.
1300 East Cliff Road
Burnsville, Minnesota 55378

Land N' Sea-Craft, Inc.
1813 South Tenth Street
San Jose, California 95112

Sea-Space Corporation
15 Berry Hill Road
Oyster Bay, New York 11771

Samson Marine Design Enterprises Ltd.
833 River Road
Richmond, B.C. Canada

INTERESTING READING

Pamphlets:

The Resources Agency
Department of Navigation & Ocean Development
Sacramento, California 95814

1. *Basic Facts About Life Preservers and Other Water Safety Devices.*
2. *Safe Boating Hints For The Southern California Coast.*
3. *Basic Facts About Marine Fire Extinguishers.*
4. *Safe Boating Hints For California Lakes and Reservoirs.*
5. *ABC's of California Boating Law.*

U.S. Coast Guard
400 Seventh Street S.W.
Washington, D.C. 20591

1. *Emergency Repairs Afloat* - The Boatman's pocket guide to: Engine trouble shooting, emergency repairs, How to stay afloat, recommended Basic Handtools and Spare parts.

Books:

Navigation:

Primer of Navigation, by George Mixter, Van Nostrand-Reinhold, 450 W. 33rd St., New York, New York 10001
How to Navigate Today, Cornell Maritime Press Inc., Box 109, Cambridge, Maryland 21613
Piloting, Seamanship, Small Boat Handling, Charles E. Chapman

General Interest:

The Foxfire Book (lots of home-made recipes, how-to-do-things by hand, etc.), The Southern Highlands Literary Fund, Rabun Gap, Georgia 30568

Solar Energy:

Direct Use of the Sun's Energy, Farrington Daniels, 1964
Basic Sailing, M.B. George, Motor Boating & Sailing, Revised edition. Hearst Corp., 959 8th Avenue, New York, New York 10009
Unknown Horizon - A book about strange sea phenomena.
Marinship Coloring Book, P.O. Box 617, Sausalito, California 94965

Magazine publications:

Ocean Living, Box 17463, Los Angeles, California 90017
Family Houseboating, P.O. Box 2081, Toluca Lake, California 91602
Hydroponics as a Hobby, Growing Plants Without Soil, c / o Cooperative Extension Service, University of Illinois at Urbana-Champaign, Urbana, Illinois 61801

The Wonderful World of Houseboating

Supplies the would-be houseboater with the information and instruction he'll need to rent a houseboat, or purchase one for a floating home. Newcomb describes the many types available and how to furnish, accessorize and navigate them. He explains how to rent a houseboat and includes a list of rental agencies, how to plan a trip and what to bring along, and so forth. A useful feature of this heavily illustrated book is a special map section with seven regional maps that show at a glance where houseboating may be done in the U.S., and 21 detailed maps zero in on some of the "hot spots" around the country. All in all a very good source of information for houseboating types.

—AP

The Wonderful World of Houseboating
Duane Newcomb
1974; 204pp.

$9.95 postpaid

from:
Prentice-Hall, Inc.
Box 500
Englewood Cliffs, NJ
07632

or Whole Earth

In buying a houseboat, as in renting one, your primary consideration should be *how you intend to use it.* If you want a getaway family boat for leisurely weekend cruising, stick to the pontoon models. Several manufacturers produce this kind of craft, with prices ranging from $4500 to $13,000, and lengths from 18 to 50 feet. All models are powered by outboard motors and can do from 6 to 12 miles per hour. Interiors are pleasantly comfortable.

Should you prefer something that can handle long cruises with ease, really moves and looks more like a conventional boat, consider the cruiser hulls. Conventional hull types come in steel, aluminum and fiberglass. They are powered by single- or twin-engine inboards and reach speeds of over 30 mph. Prices range from $6995 to over $50,000, and sizes from 30 to 59 feet. Numerous livability features and a wide variety of interior designs are available, with a trend toward sleeker exteriors.

CREDITS

Cover art, Bill Oetinger
Photos, pp. 12 (upper), 32 (lower), 39, 45 (upper), 63 (lower): J. Woods
Photo, pg. 33 (upper): Marty
Photo, pg. 50: Stephen Siskind
Photo, pg. 67: Edward E. Caine
Etching, pp. 92-3: Joy Fibben
Map, pg. 109: *Bay Guardian*
Photos, pp. 111, 113: Wolfe Worldwide Films
Photos, pp. 112, 116: Chong Lee
Photos, pp. 126, 127: A.C. Rippolone
Photos, pg. 107 (upper): Pat Stone

First printed in April 1975
at Anderson, Ritchie & Simon, Los Angeles;
covers by Haagen Printing, Santa Barbara;
composition by Mackintosh Typography, Santa Barbara;
laid out by Noel Young and Patty Yancey.

BEVERLY DUBIN began this book while doing graduate work at Lone Mountain College in San Francisco, where she now lives. Writer, artist, and photographer, she has traveled extensively throughout America and co-authored the book, "Roll Your Own" in 1974.

127

Noah built the first houseboat.

Cleopatra floated down the Nile
on a houseboat.